spot

HORSES

QUARTER HORSES

by Alissa Thielges

AMICUS

blaze

race

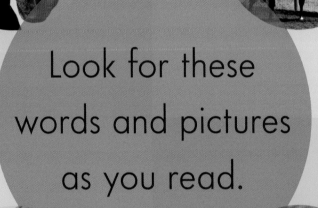

Look for these
words and pictures
as you read.

hind legs

rope

What a strong horse!
It is a quarter horse.

blaze

See the blaze?
It is a face marking.
It is a wide stripe.

race

See the race?
A quarter horse sprints.
It is fast in short races.

A quarter horse works hard.
It is used on ranches.
It helps move the cows.

See the hind legs?
They are powerful.
They turn quickly.

hind legs

See the rope?
The calf is caught.
This horse is good
in roping events.

rope

A quarter horse is calm.
It is great with kids.
Let's ride!

blaze

See the blaze?
It is a face marking.
It is a wide stripe.

race

See the race?
Quarter horse sprints.
It is fast in short races.

Did you find?

hind legs

See the hind legs?
They are powerful.
They turn quickly.

hind legs

rope

See the rope?
The calf is caught.
This horse is good
in roping events.

rope

spot

Spot is published by Amicus
P.O. Box 227, Mankato, MN 56002
www.amicuspublishing.us

Library of Congress Cataloging-in-Publication Data
Names: Thielges, Alissa, 1995– author.
Title: Quarter horses / by Alissa Thielges.
Description: Mankato, Minnesota : Amicus, [2023] | Series:
    Spot horses | Audience: Ages 4–7 | Audience: Grades
    K–1 | Summary: "Meet the quarter horse breed in this
    leveled reader that reinforces key vocabulary with a
    search-and-find feature. Carefully controlled text and
    excellent photos introduce these fast, powerful horses to
    early readers."–Provided by publisher.
Identifiers: LCCN 2021055487 (print) | LCCN 2021055488
    (ebook) | ISBN 9781645492481 (hardcover) | ISBN
    9781681527727 (paperback) | ISBN 9781645493365
    (ebook)
Subjects: LCSH: Quarter horse–Juvenile literature.
Classification: LCC SF293.Q3 T45 2023 (print) | LCC SF293.
    Q3 (ebook) | DDC 636.1/33–dc23/eng/20211213
LC record available at https://lccn.loc.gov/2021055487
LC ebook record available at https://lccn.loc.
    gov/2021055488

Rebecca Glaser, editor
Deb Miner, series designer
Catherine Berthiaume and Grant Gould,
book design and photo research

Photos by Shutterstock/Vera Zinkova
cover 1, 16, Kwadrat 3, Bob Pool 14–15;
Alamy/Tierfotoagentur 4–5, Mark Shahaf
6–7, imageBROKER 8–9, Yaacov Dagan
10–11, Luc Novovitch 12–13

QUARTER HORSES